Dating Quilts

FROM 1600
TO THE
PRESENT

by Helen Kelley

Design and production
coordination by
Bonnie Smetts Design

Portions of this book
were previously
self-published and
copyrighted by the
author in 1985.

Published by C&T
Publishing, P.O. Box
1456, Lafayette,
California 94549

ISBN 0-914881-95-7

Library of Congress Cataloging-in-Publication Data

Kelley, Helen (Helen L.)
    Dating quilts : from 1600 to the present / by Helen Kelley.—
1st ed.
        p.   cm.
    Includes bibliographical references (p. 60).
    ISBN 0-914881-95-7
    1. Quilts—United States—Dating. 2. Quilts—United States—
Identification. I. Title.
NK9112.K45 1995
746.46'0488—dc20   94-38760

This material is compiled from a variety of sources. It has been gleaned from every reliable printed source that I could discover, and I have assiduously stored away gems from the minds of historians that I greatly admire for their scholarly research and religious attention to accuracy. Much information has been gained from my own quilt exposure. At first, my notes were scratchily written in a small notebook that I treasured and carried with me. I have translated here my own barely legible handwriting and miserably typed records to help you accurately assess and record America's quilt treasures. This book is indexed and portable. Make notes of your own on these pages as your experience grows and your understanding of quilts increases.

Introduction

Research continually yields new textile facts. The clues listed on these pages are not absolutes— at least most of them are not. Obviously a machine-stitched quilt will not predate the marketing of the sewing machine, and brilliant aniline colors will not be found prior to Mr. Perkins' discovery of mauve dye, the event that led to the development of these pigments. Even that information is subject to interpretation, however. A machine-stitched binding could have been applied to an older quilt at a more recent date, and some dyes are fugitive and difficult to identify once they have faded. An innovative quilter may well have created a quilt design that was ahead of her time, and many styles that were popular at a specific time lingered across the years to be repeated as the decades slipped by.

Too, there is the question of quilts that are multi-generational, begun by one quiltmaker and handed down across the years to be stitched on by successive quilters. Look, too, at quiltmakers who collected and cached away fabric scraps over a span of years, all to be used in the same quilt. My favorite quandary is this: Consider my own wedding quilt, made in 1948 from a kit that was produced around 1920. What sort of a date would you put on that quilt?

Some clues are so strong that the moment you unfold the quilt, it's as if somebody pulled the light chain and illuminated the inside of a dark closet. I remember walking into a merchants' mall in North Carolina and seeing across the room a quilt printed with the magnificent old Prussian blue dye. I was drawn to that quilt as if it were singing a siren's song, and I was thrilled when, some years later, Erma Kirkpatrick of Chapel Hill, North Carolina, saw the picture I had taken of it, and she gasped, "That's my quilt! I bought that quilt!" I felt gratified that a kind lady I knew had taken in that lovely "orphan" and cared for it.

I am fond of telling people that you have to look at a quilt and listen to the music, the whole song. Some individual fabric is very identifiable, but the true melody is in the chords created by the combination of materials. The old reds and blues from the early years of the 20th century are much easier to identify when they "sing" together. Tell me, too, what you think when you unfold a quilt and discover that it is a blend of soft browns or a display of strong gold, green, and red? Do little spots sound a musical clue—perhaps, cottonseed stains, blood stains, or iron-water marks?

I am constantly learning. I learn something from every quilt I see. I ask questions: "Where did this quilt come from? Do you know anything about the maker? Have you any idea about the origins of this fabric, this quilt pattern?" Then, I note these things in my book. Already it has fresh scrawls on its pages.

HLK

Dedication
To my mother and my father

Acknowledgments
Marcia Anderson, Cuesta Benberry, Shiela Betterton, Barbara Brackman, Mary Ann Butterfield, Carol Crabb, Helen Fetzer, Sally Garoutte (1925-1989), Joyce Gross, Bettina Havig, Dolores Hinson, Dorothy Stish

STYLES *(Trends and Fads)*

`1600-1830`

Chintz Cut-Outs

Applied with overcast stitch, blindstitch
or fine buttonhole stitch in white or
unbleached thread

Whole-Cloth Quilts

Colors or print fabrics (*i.e.* chintzes)

Frequently quilted on heavy batting

Marseilles Quilting

Quilted in France and exported

Two layers, no padding

Corded and stuffed

Earliest were corded with unbleached roving

1775-1800

One Patch Quilts

Medallion Quilts

Large whole-cloth centers

Sometimes with large stars, sunbursts or printed handkerchiefs at the center

All-White Quilts

After the development of the cotton spinning, weaving industry in America (Cotton gin invented in 1793)

1800-1840

Stenciled Quilts

Development of a number of geometric quilt blocks that were in continual use from this time on

1840-1860

Album Quilts

Presentation, Friendship, Autograph,
Brides, Baltimore Album Quilts date from
1845–1855

1840-1850

Medallion Quilts using loomed Marseilles spreads for background

The Jacquard loom on which these
Marseilles spreads were manufactured arrived
in America in 1820

1850-1860

Sewing machine in general use

Mass-marketed in 1856

Sometimes threaded in contrasting thread

1850-1880

Four Block Quilts

Four identical, large squares such as Princess Feathers, Bouquets, Eagles

1860-1900

Silhouette Quilts

Flags, Fans, Schoolhouses, Butterflies, Horseshoes, Botanicals, Profiles

Log Cabins

1861-1865: The Lincoln Years

Civil War Quilts

Union quilts frequently had eagles

Confederate quilts often were appliquéd with flowers

Crazy Patch

Wools, Silks and Satins

Autograph Quilts with the names of famous people

Frequently embroidered in red thread

Sometimes arranged with names radiating from a circle

Many were fund raisers

Scripture Quilts

1875-1900

Kate Greenaway Designs

Sunbonneted girls and other outlined figures (embroidered)

Stenciled Quilts revived

1876

Centennial Quilts

1880-

Quotation Quilts

1880-1900

Wool Patch tobacco premiums, cigar bands, tobacco pouch labels

Charm Quilts

No two pieces of the same fabric

Pieces set in one-patch designs such as Tumblers, Pyramids, Brick-Work, Mosaics (hexagons), Diamonds, Small Four Patches, and Nine Patches

Note: Many pieced patterns fell into disuse during this time due to the rage for silk and velvet Victoriana.

1900

The decline of Victoriana

Crazy Patches became less artistic

Embroidery was less varied, frequently employing only feather stitching

Silk Novelties

Cigar Bands

Cigarette Premiums such as flags

Labels

Silk Cushions
Made in Log Cabin, Rail Fence, Hexagons

1910-

A return to the quaint "Cottage" and "Colonial" styles

1914-

Kindergarten Blocks
9" stamped blocks for red embroidery

European War Relief Quilts

1915-

Floral Appliqué
Marie Webster's book, *Quilts: Their Story and How To Make Them*, published with many floral appliqué designs

STYLES

Kit Quilts

Commercial designs in patterns and kits available in stores and by mail order

Perforated quilting patterns available

Red Cross Quilts

"Mountain Quilts"

Made by remote Appalachian cottage industries

1917-

World War I: "Quilts for the Boys"

Liberty Quilts for the home front

U.S. Government used wool crop for blankets for the servicemen

Much red, white, and blue

Ruby Short McKim patterns first published

1918-

World War I ends

Poppy quilts
  "In Flanders fields, the poppies blow."

Quilting taught as therapy to returning wounded

1919-

Quilts for Devastated France

All-White Quilts featured in magazines

1920-

Leaves and Botanical Quilts

Silhouettes

Floral Quilts
  Frequently applied with fine buttonhole
  stitches in matching-color thread

Charm Quilts revived

1920-1930

Silk, Rayon or Sateen Whole-Cloth Quilts offered as high-priced items by cottage industries

Floral Appliqués, Kits, and Patterns available from many sources

Postage Stamp Quilts

Yo-Yo Coverlets

Embroidered automobiles, boats, trollies, airplanes, lilypads, children under umbrellas (in red or blue threads)

1930-

Depression Quilts

The financial market had collapsed in 1929

Quilts of dress and apron scraps

Frequently these quilts had no borders, since they were less likely to have large pieces of purchased fabrics

Sunbonnets

Black blanket-stitching popular around appliquéwork

Charm Quilts set in designs other than One Patches, sometimes with alternate plain blocks

Newspaper Pattern Series published under such names as "Laura Wheeler," "Nancy Cabot," and "Alice Brooks"

Pockets of identifiable regional quilts flourished

Lancaster County Amish quilts

Southern African-American quilts

A group of Kansas quiltmakers whose masterful appliqué quilts were unique

1940-

Quilting waned when America went to war again, with housewives working in defense industries

1975-

Quilting blossomed once again with the advent of the Bicentennial

Patriotic Quilts

Log Cabin Quilts

Old quilt tops found in attics were quilted at this time

Grandmother's Flower Garden

Dresden Plate

Sampler Quilts

Baltimore Album Revival Quilts

Wall Hangings (smaller size)

A new awareness of the creative possibilities inherent in quilts

FABRICS

1775-1800

Block Prints

Small stylized florals

Browns, purples, and reds

Floral trails, some with pindots or picotage

Dark-ground Prints

Resist-dyed Fabrics in one or two shades of blue

Floral Stripes printed in red and black with a third color penciled in (yellow, blue or green, which was yellow/blue together)

Hewson Print Centers

    Fine prints in madder colors

Chintz

    Overpainted in five or more colors to achieve a variety of hues

Copperplate Prints
(English and French)

Monochromes only

Red, blue, black or purple
Purples frequently changed over time to
brown or sepia

Solids

Worsteds, druggets, twills, silks, etc.

Checks and Plaids

1800-1825

Block Prints

Polychrome-striped Florals

Pillar Prints with flowery capitals

Lapis Prints

Colors were printed next to and touching
each other without areas of white between

Red, blue

Pompeian Prints

> *The Last Days of Pompeii* by Edward George Earle Lytton Bulwer-Lytton, 1st Baron
>
> Use of red, yellow, and black

Roller Prints

1815: Earliest roller prints were printed in a single color with extra colors added by woodblock

New strong shades:

> 1817 Antimony orange
>
> 1823 Manganese brown

Drab-style Prints

Absence of reds and purples

Yellow, buff, brown, olive used

Acorns, oak leaves, thistles, bunches of clustered flowers

Shawl Prints

Small repeats using Indian and Paisley shawl motifs

Palm Trees and Wild Game Birds

Chinoiserie Designs (Chinese)

Discharge Prints

Indigo Grounds

Minute Pinwork (white dots)

1825-1850

Rainbow Prints

Variety of ground colors in vertical stripes

Fondue Prints

Streaking of a single color

Motifs printed on top of shading

Fancy Machine Grounds

All-over trellis ground

All-over pin ground

All-over dotted, diapered, netted and honey-combed grounds

Cracked-Ice grounds

Small-Scale Active Designs

Reds, blues, greens, browns

Coral-like forms

Little sprays and dots

Curly leaves with tattered edges

Sprigs with berries

Fine jagged forms in eccentric geometric squiggles

These shapes are stylized designs printed on elaborate grounds

Victorian Ornamentation

Particularly 1840-1850

Meandering scrollwork

Arabesques, cartouches

New Colors

Pistachio, lavender, lime green, blue-green

Heavy use of brown, rose, green, and purple

Shawl Prints (continuation of)

Checks

Plaids

FABRICS

Floral Stripes

Polka Dots

Orange background with black dots

Dots can be large and small, sparse or crowded

Pillar Prints reappear

Roller Prints

1825–1830: With two rollers red and black inked together

After 1840: Many colors together

1850-1875

A variety of sharp, bright colors

The new aniline dyes

Orange-toned Paisley imitations

1870s: Coppery-red, orange, brown, white, and black together

Prints that imitated woven goods

Plissé, matelassé, moiré

White Grounds with tiny printed designs on shirting fabric

Red, brown, blue, black

Triangles, squares, circles

Other designs: Stick pins, horseheads, foxheads, stirrups, nails and sledge hammers, ants and flies, dominoes, small crescents, little girls and boys

Small patterned flowers

Likely to have no leaves or stems

Outlines in black

Simulated Patchwork

Centennial Prints

Bells, shields, flags, eagles, George Washington

Challis used quite extensively

Navy-blue Grounds patterned in white, red or yellow

FABRICS

Purple Grounds and soft grays
Printed in white or black

Checks and Plaids

1875-1900

Shirting Fabric Prints
Not so fussy or detailed and minute

Slightly larger scale
Red, white, navy-blue

Anchors, bells, grids, springs, bubbles, circles (concentric and also interlocking)

Larger horseheads, horseshoes, riding whips, foxheads, stirrups

Commemorative Fabrics

One design in many colors available
Gray, mauve, blue, rose, rust, etc.

1900-1915

Designs appear to have been influenced by the Bauhaus movement in art

Clean lines, simple, curved shapes

Art Deco quality to many of the geometrics

Quilts were often dominated with reds and blues early in this period

Rayon appears

First manufactured in America in 1910

1915-

Pastels or livelier colors

Fuchsia, peach, coral, aqua on a white ground

Representational Prints

Less detail

Larger scale designs

Sateens

FABRICS

Continuation of Calicoes of the 19th century

Less delicacy

Percales in vivid solid colors

Pink, Nile green, yellow, red, orange, lavender, and blue

1925-

Feed and Flour Sack Prints

1940-

Strong colors and large scale geometrics and plaids

Orange, black, blue, yellow, green

1960-

Bright-colored Percales of the earlier years still available

The fabric market flooded with blends

Polyester Double Knits

1975-

Bicentennial Fabrics

A proliferation of printed cotton fabrics made specifically with the quilter in mind

Coordinated colors

Floral Stripes

Prints to imitate hand-dyed art fabrics

Fabrics hand-dyed by the quilter

Reproduction Prints to imitate historic fabrics

FILLERS

Cotton Batts

These have been used for centuries. It is not possible to determine age of quilts from these fillers.

To this day, cotton batts can still be obtained both bleached and unbleached. Some contain dross from the preparation process.

Most of today's commercially prepared batts, however, are clean, white, even, and bonded with resin.

Wool Batts

Like cotton batts, these have been used for centuries, and it is not possible to determine age from such fillers.

30

Many early wool batts were hand-prepared.

Today, there are carding machines commercially available to card old wool batts.

Contemporary wool fillers are frequently luxurious, even batts.

Polyester Batts

First marketed in 1955 by Mountain Mist (Stearns & Foster Company, now Stearns Technical Textiles Company).

Blankets

Cotton flannel in use since the 1870s.

Note: Exploring the filling of an old quilt will sometimes reveal that an even older, worn quilt has been used as a filler.

QUILT SIZES

1700-1830

Large Beds. Sometimes 3 to 4 yards wide, requiring quilts 108" x 108" or 144" x 144"

1825-1850

3/4 Beds. 6 feet to 7 1/2 feet square, requiring quilts 78" x 78" or 90" x 90"

1900s

For Double Beds: Increased size of quilts to 7 feet or 8 feet, *i.e.* 84" x 84" or 96" x 96"

For Twin Beds: 72" x 90" or 96"

Note: Quilts made in the second half of the 20th century have variable measurements due to the variety of beds in use: queen-size, king-size, water beds, etc., and the use of quilts as wall decorations from small to large for home and commercial installations.

BORDERS & EDGES

1700s and early 1800s

Loomed-tape binding

Narrow, straight-grain binding

1800-1825

Three-sided borders

Before 1850

Netting and hand-woven fringe

Elaborately quilted borders

1840-1880

Piped edges

BORDERS & EDGES

Victorian

Lace, Pearls, Ribbons

1900-

Narrow, bias binding

Commercially packaged bias tapes first
marketed in 1897 by William E. Wright

1950-

**A tendency for $1/2$" or wider
binding, both straight-grain and bias**

**Double-fold or French binding
probably indicates a contemporary
quilt**

Note: The binding of a quilt is not a reliable indicator of
its age since many frayed older quilts have been rebound
to preserve their beauty and/or serviceability.

PATTERNS

Before 1825

Early patterns included Stars, Pine Trees, 1000 Pyramids

1825-1850

Lady of the Lake
Poem written by Sir Walter Scott in 1810

1840

Moss Rose and Whig Rose

1844

Whig's Defeat

1885-1900

Kate Greenaway
   Often embroidered in Turkey red thread

Sunbonnets that resembled Dutch Cleanser girls

1918-1919

Red Cross Quilts

1920s and '30s

Sunbonnet Revival

Grandmother's Flower Garden

Dresden Plate

Double Wedding Ring

Pieced Butterflies and Flowers

SIGNATURES

1800-

Early quilts were frequently cross-stitched

This tradition has been carried across the years

1830-

Signed in ink

Indelible ink introduced 1830

1840-1870

Stencils and stamps

Earlier ones have designs such as Plumes, Eagles, etc.

Later ones have more basic block letters

Quilted Signatures

Can sometimes be discovered by holding a light above the quilt so that it casts a shadow across the quilting

1900-

Penned and embroidered signatures continued

1976-

Labels made with

Sewing-machine embroidery

Photographic prints on cloth

Embellished block design from front of quilt

Elaborate appliqué

Name, date, and copyright marks sometimes on face of quilt

PRINTING TECHNIQUES

Until 1775

Wood Blocks

Patterns were about 10" long

Some colors "penciled" in

1755

Wood Blocks

Introduction of Copperplate Printing

Plates were up to 36" square with large scale designs printed in a single color

Delicate lines and fine printing in red, blue, black or purple

1783

Copperplate Printing
Includes English and French *toiles de Jouy*

Roller Printing was developed
Design: 28" wide. Repeat: 12"
Technique in general use by 1850

1800

Roller Printing
Discharge Printing
Resist Printing

Woodblock Monochromes

1900

Roller Printing predominates

DYES

Through 1850

Natural Dyes were in common use

These included blue (woad); yellow (weld);
red, black, purple, and brown (madder); indigo

1810

"Solid Green" was developed

Before this time, green was achieved with
over-printing. Yellow or blue was applied
as a base and over-printed with the second
color to achieve green. Over-printing can
be detected in poor registry (overlapping of
lines in the printing)

1820

Mineral Dyes were developed

They were strong, acid colors: Antimony orange; Manganese bronze; Chrome yellow; Solid green

Also developed were gentler colors

Cochineal pink; Prussian blue; Catechu brown

1829

Turkey Red

Sometimes called "oiled red"

This was a fast red dye that has, in most cases, remained bright to this day

Other Reds of this period often faded to rose

Greens often faded to pea-green

1856

Mauve Dye

Discovered by Perkins during his coal
tar research. Led to the development of
aniline dyes

1870

Coppery-colored Dyes

1900

Navy-blues and Reds dominated

1920-1940

Flower colors

Lavender, yellow, pink, and Nile green
(sometimes referred to as "poison green")

1950

Fluorides, called "brighteners," were in general use as additives to both dyes and detergents, replacing old blueing products

Note: A "black light" (ultra violet) is a valuable tool for discovering if contemporary fabric has been used to restore old quilts. A fluorescent ultra violet tube (GE F4T5 BLB®) can be ordered from lighting fixture wholesalers and retailers. Two of these small tubes can be inserted into a fluorescent camping lantern. When this light is directed at a quilt in a darkened room, new fabrics that have been treated with fluorides, will glow.

CARE & REPAIR

Should I clean this old quilt?

❖ **Remove dirt?**

❖ **Remove age spots?**

❖ **Remove pencil marks?**

Unless the quilt is threatened by the dirt on it or by insects, no cleaning is recommended. Aged fabric is fragile. Cleaning spots will most likely remove the fabric rather than the spot. Blood spots may contain iron, which will deteriorate the fabric. Dirt may contain damaging oils or acids.

It is especially important that you not take your quilt to a dry cleaner. Some older fabrics cannot withstand today's chemicals without fading or changing color. The dry-cleaning process immerses your quilt in a fluid and agitates it. The fluid abuses your quilt and may not be totally removed. Also, even in reliable cleaning shops, one risks theft.

If you must wash your quilt, soak it in a large washing machine using a preparation obtained from a quilt store specifically for this purpose (Ensure™ and Orvus™ are two brands to consider.) or use dishwashing liquid that contains no bleach or brightener.

Note: Do not use dishwasher detergent. Distilled water is recommended. Agitate the wet quilt with your hands. Drain and add rinse water. Rinse well and arrange quilt to avoid strain on fabric while spinning. Spin out the water and allow to partially dry hung evenly over a line or laid out on a bedsheet on the lawn. While still damp, tumble briefly in a large dryer set on "Air" to soften. Quilts dried flat and without air circulation become crisp and may break along fold lines.

Should I repair this quilt?

✤ **Conservation: To protect and maintain a quilt; an attempt to preserve its original workmanship.**

✤ **Restoration: The process of adding new fabric in an attempt to restore a quilt to its original condition.**

CARE & REPAIR

Conservation is recommended. This process respects the craftsmanship of the original quilt-maker and maintains the historical value of the quilt. Restoration confuses the original work.

Remember these suggestions if you plan to do maintenance work on your quilt:

❖ Damaged areas can be more easily discovered by holding the quilt in front of an incandescent lamp.

❖ Listen carefully for the warning sounds of fiber breaking or "crying" as your needle pierces it.

❖ Remember that excess handling and the natural oils in your hands can be damaging.

❖ Use fine needles and 100%-cotton thread whenever possible.

❖ Overlay broken or worn areas of fabric with soft nylon tulle. This can be obtained in a variety of colors to match the underlying area. Cut the tulle to match the sides of the worn patch, and, with raw edges exposed, apply it along the seam.

Note: The bright new dyes of reproduction fabrics will not be likely to match aged fabrics in an old quilt if you attempt to restore it by adding new fabric.

Should I quilt this quilt top?

Think carefully about your reason for quilting an older top. Generally, an old quilt top does not increase in historic value if it is quilted by a contemporary quilter. If your wish is to have a quilt like the old top, you might consider making your own, perhaps of the same pattern and colors. A strong new quilt can withstand the wear and tear of everyday use.

If the quilt top has been made by a grandparent or parent, and you wish to quilt the top as a link to your heritage, you have a valid reason for adding your stitches to the family history.

Some quilts are tender keepsakes. Some quilts have historical significance. Some quilts are skillful and/or creative masterpieces. You must look at your quilt and decide where it fits into these categories—*e.g.*, is it An Important Piece? Please do not cut up ragged quilts to make toys, pillows, and clothing. If you have no place to store and cherish an old quilt, give it to a conservancy, a museum, or another quilt lover.

How should I store my quilt?

Do not wrap your quilt in plastic! This will seal in damaging moisture. A clean pillowcase or a washed, unbleached muslin cover that will allow air circulation is recommended.

To be realistic, most homes do not have adequate room to allow for proper storage of quilts. If you must store quilts folded, periodically refold them in an attempt to minimize sharp creases in the fabric that may break the threads in the future. Museums often store quilts singly and unfolded on long rollers, rolled with the quilt top side out. This prevents wrinkles from marring the top. Most homes do not have adequate space for this. You may, however, find space to store quilts folded softly and rolled on the 56"-long tubes that drapery manufacturers use for rolling fabric.

Do not store quilts unprotected in a drawer or chest. Cardboard and wood contain damaging acids. Acid-free tissue paper or washed un-bleached muslin are excellent protective barriers.

If you have an unused bed, layering unfolded quilts on top of it is perhaps the most satisfactory home storage method.

Can I hang this quilt on a wall?

There are several hanging techniques. Quilts can be hung by inserting a rod through a casing basted across the top back. A second rod casing along the bottom edge will ensure that the quilt hangs neatly.

Another easy installation employs a hanging board with a strip of Velcro™ nailed along its length. This is mounted on the wall. A matching strip of Velcro is basted along the top back of the quilt. The quilt is then pressed in place. If you use this method, refrain from removing your quilt impetuously lest you strain old and weakened fabric.

Display racks and wall-clamp fasteners are made especially for home display of quilts. They are available from quilt supply sources.

With any of these methods, you must remember that fabric tires and stretches, and it needs air circulation to prevent mold or other deterioration. If a quilt is stretched in a frame using Velcro tapes for mounting, it may eventually sag and droop. Do not mount quilts sealed inside a frame with a glass covering unless the backing of the frame will allow air to circulate. Perforated backing such as pegboard is recommended.

Hang quilts away from direct sunlight or fluorescent lighting to minimize fabric fading. Incandescent lighting is preferable. Remember that quilts become tired when they are hung. Periodically, take them down and rest them while you enjoy other quilts or artwork in the same location.

Museum recommendations suggest humidity and temperature control. Storage in a damp basement or in a hot attic will cause deterioration. Cleanliness is the best pest control. Insect repellents are not recommended. Any chemical poses a threat to the well-being of your quilt.

A final word: Attach a muslin label to the back of your quilt to identify its history.

TEXTILE TACTICS

© 1985 Helen E. Fetzer

Fiber	Approaching Flame	In Flame
Cotton	Does not fuse or shrink away from flame.	Burns without melting.
Silk	Fuses and curls away from flame.	Burns slowly with some melting.
Wool	Fuses and curls away from flame.	Burns slowly with some melting.
Rayon	Does not fuse or shrink away from flame.	Burns without melting.
Nylon	Fuses and shrinks away from flame.	Burns slowly with melting.
Polyester	Fuses and shrinks away from flame.	Burns slowly with melting; black smoke.
Acetate	Fuses away from flame.	Burns with melting.
Acrylic	Fuses away from flame.	Burns with melting.

Warning: Flame may flare. Hold fabric or thread with tongs. Have a
container of water immediately available. Inhale fumes with caution.

Removed From Flame	Ash Characteristics	Burning Odor
Continues to burn without melting.	Does not leave a knob or bead.	Smells like paper or marshmallow.
Burns very slowly; sometimes self-extinguishing.	Leaves soft, fluffy black ash.	No distinguishable smell.
Burns very slowly; sometimes self-extinguishing.	Leaves soft, fluffy, black ash.	Singed hair.
Continues to burn without melting.	Does not leave a knob or bead.	Burning paper.
Usually self-extinguishing.	Leaves hard tough gray round beads.	Chemical.
Usually self-extinguishing.	Leaves hard, tough, black round bead.	Chemical; perfume.
Continues to burn with melting.	Leaves brittle black, irregular-shaped bead.	Vinegar.
Continues to burn with melting.	Leaves hard, brittle, black irregular-shaped bead.	Chemical.

Aniline Dyes: A wide range of brilliant synthetic dyes, more colorfast than natural dyes.

Dictionary

Bonding: A process of smoothing out a quilt batting and spraying it with a thin layer of resin to prevent the batting from bearding through fabrics in a quilt.

Broderie Perse: Late-19th century. A technique in which chintz designs were cut out, pasted with a mixture of flour, water, and alum to a base fabric and then applied with a buttonhole stitch and embellished with embroidery. Also called "Cretonne Work."

Carding: A preliminary process for removing impurities and some short, broken or immature fibers in wool or cotton, as well as combing out or straightening the fibers. Usually this is done by a card, which is a hand or mechanical instrument that has iron teeth or wires, and is used in pairs.

Calico: Originally a cotton fabric from India, painted, printed, glazed or plain. In the 20th century, a cotton fabric printed with a small floral design.

Challis: A soft fabric, originally of wool, but now of varied fibers, often printed with Persian flower designs.

Cheater Cloth: 20th-century term identifying fabric printed with imitation patchwork designs. See also Simulated Patchwork.

Chintz: A glazed-cotton fabric, originally from India. Usually printed with floral designs and garden scenes.

Chintz Appliqué: A 300-year-old technique in which chintz designs are cut out and applied, originally to full bed quilts, and later to quilt blocks.

Conversation Prints: 20th-century term for small, fanciful prints of the late-19th century.

Cretonne: A furnishing fabric with large designs used for draperies and slipcovers. Unglazed chintz.

Crying: The characteristic noise made when metals are bent. When applied to fabrics, this term means a faint cracking or sighing sound sometimes heard when fabric is brittle and old. This sound gives notice that a quilt needs extremely gentle handling.

Dimity: A heavy cotton with a linen warp, sometimes striped or checked.

Discharge Printing: Printing with a bleach to remove color of dyed fabric and produce a white design. Design was sometimes reprinted with a second color.

Double Pink: 19th-century print in tiny patterns. Sometimes called "rose pink" or "cinnamon pink." Contemporary: "bubblegum pink."

Dross: Waste matter or refuse such as seeds, dirt, or twigs found in some cotton batting, which has not been thoroughly cleaned.

Drugget: A fabric of wool or mixed fibers. Described by historians as thin and narrow.

Fustian: A heavy fabric, cotton or wool, sometimes with a nap. Cotton fustian was used for linings, undergarments, and bed curtains.

Ground: Basic design area of a fabric, the background, upon which a larger pattern is frequently printed.

Handkerchiefs: Printed in the 19th century with floral, religious or patriotic themes. Used as quilt centers.

Hewson, John: Opened a printworks in Philadelphia in 1774 where he produced woodblock prints of exceptional quality. Quilts with Hewson panels are museum treasures today.

Lapis Red and Lapis Blue: Early-19th-century dye process that allowed red and blue areas to be dyed adjacent to each other without white space between them.

Linsey-Woolsey: By definition is a fabric of half linen, half flax. The recorded fiber contents, however, are indefinite. Today, early, all-wool quilts are sometimes referred to by this name.

Madder: An ancient dye, a product of the madder plant, producing reds ranging from orange to rusty red to ruby.

Marseilles Quilting: 18th-century all-white quilting, corded and stuffed; produced in the south of France.

Marseilles Spreads: 19th-century spreads woven on Jacquard looms to imitate the earlier quilting.

Matelassé: A loomed fabric of two or more layers having the appearance of quilting.

Moiré: A finish applied to fabric, (cotton, silk, etc.) to give the appearance of water-marking.

Muslin: Originally, a downy cotton fabric from India; may be bleached or unbleached.

Palampore: A painted Indian panel, often with a flowering tree design, used on early European and American medallion quilts.

Pencilling: Hand-painted additional colors on block print designs.

Percale: A fine woven cotton dress fabric, now obtainable in a variety of widths. Until recently frequently found in 36" widths.

Picotage: Characterized by tiny dots to give shading and interest to design. Sometimes called "Pinning."

Plissé: A fabric treated (in stripes) with a caustic soda to cause shrinking and produce a crinkled effect.

Resist Printing: Printing with a wax or paste to resist dye in the dye bath, *i.e.*, batik. Also, the binding off of portions of fabric to shield them from the dye bath, *i.e.*, tie dying.

Roving: Spun yarn sometimes called "cording" or "wicking."

Simulated Patchwork: Late-19th-century term denoting fabric printed in patchwork designs. See also Cheater Cloth.

Stuffed Quilting: An old term applied to quilts whose design lines and shapes have been padded with roving or cotton wadding. 20th-century terms: "Italian Quilting" or "Trapunto."

Toile: Includes a variety of fabric. Of interest to the quilter is the toile that was originally printed with copper plates in the last quarter of the 18th century. The designs were fine-lined monochromes.

Twill: A fabric characterized by woven diagonal ridges. Includes gabardine, denim, and ticking fabrics.

Vermicular: 18th century, a fine pindot ground sometimes applied to a fabric before it was block printed.

Vermiculite: 20th-century term to describe a number of tiny seaweed-like patterns from the mid-19th century usually printed in "double pink."

Worsted: A hard wool fabric.

Affleck, Diane L. Fagan. *Just New from the Mills, Printed Cottons in America*. North Andover, MA: Museum of American Textile History, 1987.

Brackman, Barbara. *Clues in the Calico*. McLean, VA: EPM Publications, Inc., 1989.

Brackman, Barbara. *Dating Antique Quilts: 200 Years of Style, Pattern and Technique*. San Francisco, CA: American Quilt Study Group, Guide No. 4, 1990.

Brackman, Barbara. *Encyclopedia of Appliqué*. McLean, VA: EPM Publications, Inc, 1993.

Brackman, Barbara. *Encyclopedia of Pieced Quilt Patterns*. Paducah, KY: American Quilter's Society, 1993.

Burns, Marilyn and Richards, Lynne. *Heirloom Textiles: Conservation and Care in the Home*. Stillwater, OK: Oklahoma State Extension Service, 1990.

Fennelly, Catherine. *Textiles in New England, 1790-1840*. Sturbridge, MA: Old Sturbridge Village Inc., 1961.

For Further Reading

FOR FURTHER READING

Florence, Cathy Gaines. *Collecting Quilts*. Paducah, KY: American Quilter's Society, 1985.

Gross, Joyce, Editor. *Quilters' Journal*. Vols. 1-31. Mill Valley, CA: Self-published, 1977-1987.

Gutcheon, Jeffrey. "Fabric Properties: Color Loss and Cleaning." *Quilter's Newsletter Magazine,* Reader Service Leaflet No. 12. Wheat Ridge, CO., 1985.

Gutcheon, Jeffrey. "Fabric Properties: Thread Count, Blends, & Finishes." *Quilter's Newsletter Magazine,* Reader Service Leaflet No. 13. Wheat Ridge, CO., 1985.

Kiracofe, Roderick. *The American Quilt*. New York, NY: Clarkson Potter, Pub., 1993.

Khin, Yvonne M. *The Collector's Dictionary of Quilt Names and Patterns*. New York, NY: Portland House, 1988.

Mailand, Harold F. *Considerations For the Care of Textiles and Costumes, A Handbook for the Non-Specialist*. Indianapolis, IN: Indianapolis Museum of Art, 1980.

Miller, Susan and Elffers, Joost. *Textile Designs*. New York: Harry N. Abrams, Inc., Pub., 1991.

Montgomery, Florence M. *Printed Textiles, English and American Cottons and Linens 1700-1850*. New York, NY: Viking Press, 1970.

Ordonez, Margaret and Slinkman, Zoe. *Quilt Conservation*. Lawrence, KS: Kansas State University Cooperative Extension Service, 1981.

Orlofsky, Patsy and Myron. *Quilts in America*. New York, NY: McGraw-Hill, 1974; reprint: New York, NY: Abbeville Press, 1992.

Pettit, Florence H. *America's Printed and Painted Fabrics 1600-1900*. New York, NY: Hastings House, 1970.

Puentes, Nancy O'Bryant. *First Aid for Family Quilts*. Wheat Ridge, CO: Moon Over the Mountain Publishing Company, 1986; Leman Publications, Inc., 1992.

Uncoverings: Research Papers of the American Quilt Study Group. San Francisco, CA.: AQSG, 1980- (Published annually).

Swan, Susan Burrows. *Plain and Fancy, American Women and Their Needlework, 1700-1850*. New York, NY: Holt, Rinehart and Winston, 1977.

Helen Kelley came by her love of fabrics quite naturally. During the 1930s, her father was a management consultant in a Georgia textile mill. Her mother was a talented needlewoman who taught Helen to sew at a tender age. From these two people, Helen inherited her father's tiny pick glass (a lens for counting threads), her mother's Rose Wreath wedding quilt, and an appreciation for meticulous detail.

About the Author

Helen married in the 1940s, and for this occasion, she made her first quilt, which was appliquéd with green and purple daisies, neatly buttonholed in place. Since that venture, Helen has moved about the United States with her husband, finally settling in Minnesota where she raised five children and made countless more quilts.

Helen's first book, *Scarlet Ribbons* (AQS), explored the needlework of Native Americans.

Quilt With the Best (Oxmoor House) featured Helen's quilting classes on a Scottish island. Her "Loose Threads" column has appeared monthly in *Quilter's Newsletter Magazine* since 1983.

Studying antique quilts became a passion for Helen as she read the stories of early quiltmakers. Each old quilt is a testimonial to one of those quilters. The fabrics, patterns, and styles of old quilts hold hints of those earlier times. If you look closely at your old quilt, finger it, and listen carefully. Perhaps it has a tale to tell you, too.

Other Fine Quilting Books are available from C&T Publishing. For more information write for a free catalog from:
C&T Publishing
P.O. Box 1456
Lafayette, CA 94549
(1–800–284–1114)